Heaven

Sharon Milne Barbour

Heavenly guidance

Copyright © 2018 by Sharon Milne Barbour - Bengalrose Healing

Published by Bengalrose Healing
Designed by Sharon Milne Barbour
Author - Sharon Milne Barbour
Book cover illustration – by CIMBart
Editors – Sharon Milne Barbour and Di Reed

All rights are reserved. No part of this book may be reproduced by any mechanical, photographic, or electrical process, or in the form of a phonographic recording, nor may it be stored in a retrieval system, transmitted, or otherwise be copied for public or private use - other than for "fair use" as brief quotations embodied in articles. The verses can be read to private or public audience. Reviews not to be written without prior written knowledge of the publisher and author. The intent of the author is only to offer information of a general nature to help you on your spiritual path. In the event you use any of the information in the book for yourself, which is your right, the author and the publisher assumes no responsibility for your actions.

For all of humanity

CONTENTS

Section 1	Mother Earth and the animal kingdom	9
Section 2	Inspire the children	40
Section 3	Healing of the heart and mind	54
Section 4	Enlighten	90
Section 5	From the stars	118
Section 6	Find your true self	129
Section 7	Messages from the angels	150
Section 8	Daily spiritual guidance	171
	About the Author	218

Sharon and her celestial friends know you will love this channeled inspirational daily guidance book, which is inspired from her guides and other star beings. She uses the contents of this book herself on a regular basis to help guide herself and others on their life's journey.

The pages are full of 100 plus inspiring verses and wisdom. There are also 44 daily guidance inspirations messages for you at the back of the book to help guide you on your life's path.

When you need inspiration or guidance, call upon this book, before you open it each day, ask your guides to guide you to the page that will help you that day. Then open the book, the message you need will before you. After you have read the message, sit quietly and take time to reflect on the message.

This book is also aimed at light workers, mediums, spiritual teachers and celebrants to help guide, inspire and heal your clients, audience or students on their spiritual path with our words.

These guidance messages will inspire your life and others and bring the help and guidance you all need on your spiritual journey.

Section 1

Mother Earth and the animal kingdom

To find joy in your heart,
go out into Mother Nature,
find time to sit and enjoy her tune,
it will sing in your heart.

Blossom

Your journeys intertwine, like a vine in a forest,
forever searching for the light above the darkness.

You will grow fresh shoots on you life's path,
branching out in to new exciting adventures.

Keep growing towards the sunlight my friends,
and except the changes your growth will bring you.

Trust in the intuition you feel with every breath
and believe your own self worth and beauty.

You are now the great vine in the forest and
you have reached for the stars, now shine.

Be strong and true, just be YOU.

A wonderful world

You cannot save the world single-handed, but you can contribute.

Have positive thoughts every day.

Think: how can I serve for the greater good?

Donate some time to a good cause.

Help Mother Earth and her environment.

Teach someone about kindness today.

Listen to those around you.

Accept each other's faults and forgive.

These are all simple thoughts and gestures.

Let them become part of your everyday lives and you will shine a light into the dark corners of your world.

If you all did this every day, imagine what a wonderful world it would become; we just need to unite and be as one.

Mother Earth

Life is like Mother Earth; you keep spinning round in time.

Both slowly changing and adapting to different situations, sustaining yourself, being nourished by food and air.

Listen to your own heartbeat and know your true self.

Listen to Mother Earth – she is reaching out to you; there is a shift, she needs to heal and you need to heal.

Find your inner light and light up the world.

Bring love and faith to the dark corners of life by speaking out; let others hear your words.

One act of kindness brightens up Mother Earth.

One fewer act of non-pollution helps cleanse her; Mother Earth sings her song; let her heal.

Scatter our love

Harness the love around you and take it into your heart. Nourish this love so it grows and envelops you.

Then scatter your love like seeds out to your fellow Humanity. As they catch the seeds they will blossom and grow.

The love seeds are carried on the winds to unseen people. They will then share their love with the world.

As the light and love grows in the shadow of humanity, the world will become one in the love and light.

No Voice

I am a living being

Unique amongst many

I roam safe in my world

I am loved and nurtured

My kind understands me

As I grow my world changes

I feel fear and see death

My parents are no longer here

I wonder in the wilderness

I am confused and alone

I am lost amongst many

But they are not my kind

My heart grows heavy

The truth hits me hard

I am alone across time

I am the last of my kind

I have a broken heart

I am growing weak

I take my last breath

My kind is now extinct

I am not part of your future

You will see me in a book

You will see me online

A memory of your time

All I ask is WHY?

The magic of the sunrise

As the sun rises in the stillness of the morn.

Mother Earth takes a breath of the divine.

The light shining across the lands.

Awaking all life old and to be born.

The silence is awakened by the light beams.

The chorus of life sings out again to you.

The stillness now has movement and a voice.

Your heart is awakened to Mother Earth's tune.

As the sun rises into the protection of the Earth.

Your spirit stretches out to feel its warmth.

Your body absorbs its life-giving energy.

You find your path and life's worth.

As the sun sinks slowly below the horizon.

The silence falls again on your spirit within.

Know, my friends, you can hear our voice.

In the silence there is love held frozen.

Sit in the silence and listen.

Hear the night sound of the universe.

Connect to the divine light beams.

You will shine, sparkle and glisten.

The raindrop

Water is the transparency of life, reflecting all it sees in its inner self. The strength you seek lies within this life-giving force of nature. It lies within the power of the wave that can knock you off balance in body and the serenity of stillness reflecting the blue sky that calms your mind.

A single drop of this life-giving force starts new beginnings for all. One drop reflecting its world around you and look inside this power. This drop has no foes, only knows the divine life force from above. Touch the raindrop, absorb its pureness of energy, and reflect.

The single drop is part of a large universal force, calling you to watch. Stand out in the rain and be cleansed, as it cleanses Mother Nature. The single raindrop reflects you, your body and inner spirit. It mirrors the divine love and light you hold in your heart.

Reflection in the lake

Imagine the majestic earth mountains, pine forests and lakes, you are sitting at the water's edge on a completely calm beautiful summers day.

The stillness of the moment, a captured picture of time held in the mind's eye. The earth, the sky and the inner spirit are reflected in to the depth of the lake.

You are held still by the beauty and wonder of this moment, if only it could carry on forever, only being disturbed by the birds overhead and the song of nature.

A silent ripple catches your eye and brings you back to your existence in time, moving you forward with your future thoughts.

These moments of serenity have helped you leave your past behind, your mind now reflecting on the wonder of what could be.

Walk back into your busy worlds, but always hold that moment of peace and calmness in your hearts to draw on when needed.

Reflection is a form of healing, look deep in to the pools of water, search your spirit within for the answers and ask us to guide you to find that inner peace in your life.

Best friends

The physical form holds the strength of Mother Earth, made up from the elements of life itself.

The physical body holds the source of the divine pure love from beyond, your shell of energy wrapping itself like a cocoon around your spirit friend within.

Your spirit friend lies protected in your human form, connecting to all of you from within and beyond.

Joy is beheld as you travel your journey together on Mother Earth. Like best friends on an adventure to bring love and kindness and a higher way of being to the Earth plane.

There is no sadness on the day these friends separate forever, only joy is found.

The physical form has served its purpose and Mother Earth accepts you back into her bosom.

Your spiritual friend, YOU, travels back home to pick up on your spirit life you had before your Earth journey.

Your physical life is never forgotten, the human essence living on in your spirit with the knowledge and wisdom gained while here on earth.

Remember, forever blessed, forever wiser and loved beyond words at all times – while joined together and separated at death of the physical form, your light will always shine.

Sparkles on the waves

Imagine you are sitting quietly on the beach, watching the sun sparkle and glisten on the water. Your mind drifts away with the tide, as the waves lap on the shore.

Where are you going? Are you drifting away from your Earth? Drifting far beyond, to a divine existence of pure love and joy.

You reach your destination and are standing on the tip of a far horizon. Will you step over this new reality or turn around and go back?

As you hesitate, an old friend's hand draws you into a world of peace and tranquility. You are in awe of the beauty and magic this place holds.

Everything you touch sparkles and glistens, you feel the touch of the divine and are at peace. But there is a distant sound of lapping water on the shore calling you back.

The tide has come in and is washing over your feet and time is forgotten. Was it a dream or did I just touch the magic of the divine?

The Beauty of the Morning

As the beauty of the morning dawns on yet another day, your world responds like a flower opening up its petals to the morning warmth of the rays of the sun.

Your spirit is ready for this next day, the next step on its path on this journey, while walking along in the warmth and the light that the sun gives your Mother Earth.

Enjoy the beauty my friends, enjoy the song of nature, look into the depths of your oceans as there is beauty hidden everywhere on your planet.

But take yourself also to the dark parts of your world where there are depths of despair still and pollution that is hidden from the human eye.

These parts of the world have not yet found the beauty and the light that opens that flower every morning that responds to the sun and lives it life as it should.

You can all help with prayer, positive thoughts, good will, and acts of kindness to change the world you are living in.

Would it not be a wonderful thing for every human being to wake up and see the beauty of the morning, not knowing any fear or dread of the day ahead, and they only ever experience love and kindness.

All humans would then be embraced with love and light and be able to fulfill your life's to its best potential, giving and receiving so much love. Imagine what your world could be like my friends.

Imagine the beauty of the morning every day, every minute of your day, every second of your day, that feeling of wonder as you take in that morning breath of freshness of the Earths dew.

So we say to you my friends take these thoughts and spread love and light out in to your world to every human being and see the beauty that lies within humanity.

A fragile world

People are fragile, even those that seem to shine.

Be careful how you treat each other my friends, as some of you keep your cracks well hidden.

Shine out love and light and heal yourself, friends and family so the cracks you all carry can heal.

Trust, you and the world will be whole again.

June

The first of June brings new blooms, hope and rays of sunshine.

Walk in Mother Nature and smell her healing scents.

Be transformed with her positive energies and vibration.

Let June heal you and bring a smile to your face.

Join as one

You are all as one.
You live in divide.
Come together as one.
Be whole and true.
Love and see as one.
Be as one and shine.

Live hand in hand.
Walk side-by-side.
Learn from each other.
Teach each other.
Support each other.
Guide each other.

Your world will be as one.
Move forward as a whole.
Do not divide each other.
Have only thoughts of love.
All knowing will be yours.
You will live as one.

IMAGINE

Imagine the world's currency is love

Imagine the world living in peace

Imagine everyone feels safe

Imagine only kindness

Imagine neighbors helping neighbors

Imagine going beyond the stars

Imagine infinite knowledge

Imagine abundance of health

Imagine Utopia on earth

Know the spirit within.

Eternity of love is yours

Your heart can break due to your love.
But love is a treasure to remember.

Love all that is around you in your life.
Look for the positive things in your world.

Love is for Eternity you have it forever.
Just open your eyes to behold love.

Eternity of love is what we all seek.
Open your eyes love is all around you.

Mother Earth is love, feel it in the air.
Walk your Earth and breath it in.

Love is in your children's innocent eyes.
Love is in your human heart.

The Bee's song

The bee jumps from flower to flower seeking the nectar of life.

Mother Earth's creations of scent and colours attract the bee's song.

The buzz of nature gives the harmony to life on Earth.

Humanity is slowly destroying this harmony that is life itself.

The simple bee does not ask for the poisons in the air.

Be the voice for nature and Mother Earths cry for help.

Let nature sing her song and find her own true balance again.

When natures balance is reached Mother Earth will be healed.

Then the bee will cover the planet giving the abundance of life.

You will all live in harmony again as one with Mother Earth.

I am plastic

I am plastic, made out of a synthetic material by humans.

I am hard, soft, flexible, and durable and molded in to any form.

I am energy frequency, molecules with no expectations.

I can be sat on, ate off or be a container for life nourishment.

I am stubborn and stay around for a long time on Earth.

I am light enough to blow in the wind many miles.

I can travel along distance in the waterways of Mother Earth.

I fill your hedgerows with various sizes, colours and forms.

I have seen parts of your earth you will never see.

I have been dropped in to the oceans and left on mountains high.

I am slowly suffocating the animals of the oceans.

I am a danger to the young humans of your world.

I am polluting the air you breathe with carbon oxide when burnt.

You have no need for me; look back in time before I came along.

You have the technology to recycle me and make me biodegradable.

You need to STOP and rid your world of me, before I wrap my self-completely around you and suffocate you.

Heal Mother Earth

We walk the paths of Earth to enjoy the Mother Earth's Realm. To take in the sights and sounds of nature, but our hearts break when we see the human waste that's clutters up the streams, a sight we do not like.

Nature tries to survive around the hidden pollution of humanity that lies within. The bin bags that hide in the darkness slowly decaying, so many are hidden from view.

Your Mother Earth is trying to adapt but is getting lost within her soul. So please we beseech thee to look within your hearts and cleanse Mother Earth of human pollution so she sparkles from within again.

We wish you to walk the paths of Mother Earth enjoying her abundance and beauty without seeing humanities pollution taking away this wish.

We want you to all be aware of what occurs day-to-day, the pollution in Earth's waters, the beaches that are covered with the plastic of humanity that's slowly choking Mother Earth.

This was never part of her plan, what else can we say but to ask all of you to stop every day and take note of the world around you. Pick up the pollution, pick up the waste, talk to others and encourage so the world can be clean and renewed.

Mother Earth wants nature to sing its best song, not to

slowly die from the germs and pollutants of humanity. So my friends please love your world around you, protect, walk and enjoy Mother Nature so she can be healed and renewed, feeling healthy, loved and singing from her soul again.

Colourful world

You can stand and look out and think you see the colour of your world.

We ask you do you see the shades of each colour?

We ask you do you see the shadows of colours around you?

We ask you do you see the beauty of the colour you see?

We ask you do you see the vibrancy of each object you seek?

Colours are pigments given by Mother Earth for nature to show off with.

Imagine there are colours you have never seen beyond your dreams.

The universe is full of vibrant colours not yet discovered.

Take a leap of faith and explore beyond your world.

Expand your minds into the energy of creation.

We will show you things you cannot imagine.

We will light up your world with colours of the divine.

Fiction or Non-fiction

Fiction is a make believe existence.

A world of fantasy and make believe.

Non-fiction is truth and the real world.

Which do you live in, do you dream of a better world.

You can all make this world a better place, which is an equal safe world.

Work as one not, against each other.

Start to today, take one step towards your fantasy world.

It will be come your reality.

A drop in the ocean

One drop of rain can ignite the dormant seed

One drop of rain can bring the dry earth hope

One drop of rain can cause the water to overflow

One drop of rain can reflect your world like a mirror

One drop of rain can ignite curiosity in the mind

One drop of rain can ripple out for all eternity

One drop of rain is part of the cycle of life

One drop of rain is the release of nature's love

One drop of rain is the hope for humanity

One drop of rain is the release of earth's love

One drop of rain is the link to living in unison

One drop of rain is the ocean of human life

All consuming world

The innocence of nature has not asked to be part of an all-consuming world.

Each creature of earth stays cocooned in its ancient knowledge of mission and survival.

Nature walks silently within your time creating life and taking life keeping balance on earth.

Every creature on earth is made with love connected with the light of the divine.

Nature's creatures do not ask for the world to be raffished by humanity.

They ask for Mother Earth to be a haven and a safe friend for all.

We ask you step back as individuals and a whole to look at the environment around you.

Place your hand on your heart to know the truth of what lies ahead if you stay on this path.

Humanity needs to change to see the path of light for Mother Earth is going to win this fight.

Section 2

Inspire the children

*The love for a child cannot be compared;
it surrounds the heart and soul.*

The future is theirs

You make the path you follow.

You can all make this world as one.

You should help and support each other.

Not tear each other down.

Your thoughts make the future.

You need to radiate positive, loving thoughts.

You need to stand up and set the example.

You need to be strong and brave.

Move forward and shine your light.

Your children are your future.

You need to listen to their innocent minds.

You need to let them change the world.

You need to show them the path of light.

Let the children shine; the future is theirs.

Your very essence is our essence, your light is our light and we all shine as one.

Remember this while you walk your life's path on Mother Earth my friends.

Teach guidance

Guidance is the key to happiness from:

Your first breathe

Your first smile

Your first steps

Your first words

Your first actions

Your first love

Your first values

Live your talk

Walk your talk

Be true to yourself

Take this forward in your life and teach others true love and guidance.

The smile

The magic of the human smile can break down all the barriers.

A smile reflects your true inner self, the truth of the moment.

The smile of the lips and the smile in your eyes you cannot hide.

The knowing smile, the satisfied smile, the smile of contentment, the shy smile, the bright smile, the first kiss smile, the loving smile and the magic of your first smile.

A smile can change someone else's day for the better.

Be that smile that changes the world and beyond.

The nurtured child

The child never walks their path of life alone, they are always protected by their mother and father in life and in the spirit realm.

The wings of angels bring them in to this world releasing their care over to you.

You nurture them to the day they spread their wings and leave your loving home. The first stage of your job is completed as their Earth Guardian Angel.

You watch from a far with joy at their achievements, sending them love every second of your day and holding them in your hearts in times of despair.

A child will always bring you joy and heart ache, but remember my friends to be proud of what you have achieved, the fact they are confident to live their lives as they should.

They will always know you are there to fall back on in times of need and your doors and arms are always open to them.

So smile and release them into your world, we will always be at their side protecting them and guiding them on their life's path. We will call on you when you are needed just listen and look for the signs.

You are the nurturer of love and the divine and we thank you for the role you have undertaken as careers of our spirit friends and being part of their journeys so far.

Remember you all depart this world and meet in the spirit realm to continue your journeys together, so do not worry of what the future might bring, just enjoy the moments of now.

You are the teacher

The first breath teaches us about life.

The first love is when you meet your soul.

The first light takes away the darkness.

The first step is the challenges we face.

The first word is about the wisdom we seek.

The first taste is about the choices we make.

The first touch is the explorer inside us.

The first look takes you to new horizons.

The first teacher brings you knowledge.

The first lesson brings you clarity of mind.

The first child listens to your philosophy.
You are the teacher.

I am the future

I am a star child full of love.

I am your future so treat me well.

Let me be me to reach my potential.

Nurture me with love and honesty.

I have great purpose on Mother Earth.

My power lies within reaching the stars.

I am a unique being the only one of me.

Treasure the child I wish to be.

The Circle of life

Think, my friends, of your life's path from the first breath you take, until you take your last. It's not a never-ending circle; there is a beginning and end while on earth.

Fill this circle of life with love, compassion, empathy, kindness and strength. Be one of life's inspirers, leaders, and the best example humanity can offer.

You have to fill your own circle up, don't think others will do it for you, my friends; this is your story and your path; live it.

As you fill your circle up, draw others into it with love and kindness. It does not matter how big your circle gets, as long as it is pure of heart and filled with true values.

So, my friends, live your life to the full, let your circle expand to touch other hearts and inspire them from your soul.

The Love for a child

The love for a child cannot be compared; it surrounds the heart and soul.

All the sunsets and rainbows cannot out shine the children born to you.

The first look into their soul completes the bond of love for life and beyond.

Division, race, loss or hate can never break the link of fate.

The children are from the divine, with the mission to bring love to mankind.

Distance or family divide cannot break the bond of instant love they provide.

Nurture all children in your world, they are the future and love to behold.

A grandmother's promise

The love I felt as I held you in my arms for the first time is beyond words.

You woke within me a new love that belongs to the stars above.

I will treasure every hug, glance, and smile, words and kiss you give.

I will be your spiritual guardian guiding your inner light as you live.

I will light the way to lead you through darkness and pain.

I will dry your tears; make you smile and your soul sing again.

I will walk beside you every day of your life holding your hand.

I promise you the bond between us will never weaken, always shining true.

My spirit is your spirit for all time and my love is eternal to you.

Forever your friend and a promise of unconditional love I can never break.

Innocence

A smile from the innocent of pure of heart can light up the darkness.

Hope lies in a baby's smile as their innocence shines into your world.

Innocence of pain and fear exists in the pure source of unconditional love.

Creativity and clarity come from a mind innocent of being ridiculed.

The knowledge of the universe can be tapped into by the pure mind.

To find your source of love and innocence connect to your soul base energy.

The path of the soul is pure, created in the innocence of unconditional love.

This connection will lead you to your truth and the innocence of creation.

Our children know only love as they smile at me.

I now know I still have much to give on this earth.

I walk my path in new grace, kindness, and love.

I will inspire and teach the awakened ones.

We will now all unite as one for the good of man.

The awakening of a new age is what I have seen.

Knowing that some suffered but all were loved.

I now move forward with trust in my heart.

Trusting my life journey to the day I depart.

Section 3

Healing of the heart and mind

Healing is a moment of time

Make a change

Today is the day I make a change.
I am moving on to new warmth and light,
I do not want to be where my heart is breaking.

Today is the day I make a change.
I know my true friends will move forward with me,
walking alongside me on my path.

Today is the day I make a change.
I will try new things; have new experiences,
I am growing in strength and love.

Today is for ME I have made the change.
My heart is lifted from the sadness it left behind,
I smile again with new trust all will be well.

Today is for YOU make the change.
Move forward; don't hold back in the past,
The future is yours, walk forward shining.

Gather your loved ones near

Hold out your arms and gather your loved ones near.

They will give you strength my friends.

They are your inspiration,
your listeners and your support network.

Their love is your love.

Your light is their light.

Blend and be as one and you will know peace.

Healing

Healing is forgiveness

Healing is accepting your past

Healing is letting go of the pain

Healing is letting others help you

Healing is listening to your self

Healing is moving on past

Healing is a teardrop

Healing is a simple smile

Healing is a hug

Healing is a moment of time

Inner healing

Inner healing comes from within the soul.

Your heart is love; your mind can be the disease.

If you let your mind run in a negative thought pattern, your body will be dragged down with it.

When negative thoughts come in, hit them out the ballpark with a big bat in your head, and think of someone you love or a favorite moment in time.

Your body will start to fill up with positive energy, lifting your inner being. This then sends positive waves round your body healing it as it goes.

Heal from within.

Fragment of time

Life is a fragment of time, healing is a moment in time.

Fragments are part of a jigsaw that can be put together again.

If the jigsaw has a piece missing, it's not far away from you.

Search the space in your heart and you will find it.

Then gently let go of pain and negativity to us.

Now place the missing piece in the jigsaw.

You are now whole and the picture on the jigsaw is complete and clear.

What do you see?

Good byes

The wave of a hand.
The smile on your face.
The warmth of your heart.
The wisdom and grace.

Your laughter in the air.
Your scent in the wind.
Your friendship to me.
Your kindness with no end.

Today you left me behind.
Today my sun does not shine.
Today my heart has a crack.
Today I know you are fine.

You shine from above.
You send us your love.
You are beyond earth.
You fly free like a dove.

I know we will meet one day.

I will feel your warmth in time.

I will see your golden smile.

I know I will be with you again.

Let go

Do not worry of what might be.

Be in the now and understand yourself.

You, today, are what matters.

Know your true self and values.

The rest will be there for the taking.

Your tomorrow will be your now.

You will now be in the past.

Let go and be at peace with yourself.

Live your life in grace.

Find your destiny

Whispers of time float around your minds, like the soft gentle wispy clouds floating on a summer breeze. They just float happily, drifting, waiting for the day they are called up on.

When you teach my friends to settle your minds, you will be able to hold out your hands in front you and gently grasp these whispers from the past.

The softness of them will surround you holding you safe and gently nudging you in the right direction.

These whispers of time are your future; the wisdom they hold is what you have lost. Find this wisdom my friends so you can fulfill you destinies.

Spark of life

A spark, a light in the dark.

A glimpse of hope.

The light casts a shadow.

The shadow stretches before you.

Always beside you.

You are the light.

We are the shadow.

Even in the dark.

Our shadow is with you.

Light your spark to see us.

Hear us and feel us.

Sparkle and shine bright.

An eternity of love is yours

An eternity of love is what we all seek.
Open your eyes – love is all around you.

Mother Earth is love, feel it in the air.
Walk your Earth and breath it in.

Love is in your children's innocent eyes.
Love is in your human heart.

Your heart can break due to your love.
But love is a treasure to remember.

Love all that is around you in your life.
Look for the positive things in your world.

Love is for eternity you have it forever.
Just open your eyes to behold love.

Your Ego

Your ego is like orange peel wrapped round you.

If you let the orange stay whole, you never get to taste the juicy fruit of life.

Learn my friends to peel back the ego and take a bite of the offerings of creation.

Once you master this, the universe and all it has to offer is yours.

So take the fruits of life, my friends and leave the peel behind.

You are one

Live as one.
You live in divide.
Come together as one.
Be whole and true.
Love and see as one.
Be as one and shine.

Live hand in hand.
Walk side by side.
Learn from each other.
Teach each other.
Support each other.
Guide each other.

Your world will be as one.
Move forward as a whole.
Do not divide each other.
Only thoughts of love.
All knowing will be yours.
You will live as one.

Who's in the mirror?

Human, flesh and bone is how you see your reflection.

Your mirror reflects back what only your eyes see.

Humanity defines themselves by what lies on top of the surface.

Step back from the mirror and look around you and beyond. Now look beyond the horizon; do this with your fellow human beings too. You are truly defined by what lies beneath what you cannot see.

You are all more than just a reflection, a glance in a mirror. Look down deep within your own body; get to know yourself. When you know what defines you, you will judge others in a different way.

Now you see human, flesh, bone, spirit, pure essence and love. Now your reflection in the mirror has expanded to the fill the room. Your soul now shines out from the mirror to reflect around the world.

You are in the mirror, my friend.

Friendship

Friendship is a bond held within the boundaries of the heart and within in the rings of time.

We see your hearts break when these bonds are broken, an unseen force causing separation and distance.

Sometimes reasons for loss are never known, it is part of your path and the lost friend holds the truth, as this is their learning journey too.

But with destiny sometimes words and actions will never rekindle that friendship that's lost, so except this and move on with your life.

Then you have the friendships that stand the test of time; always a heartbeat away for the connection to rekindle.

These friends are your true soul connections the ones here to guide, love and protect you no matter the distance that stands between you.

Treasure these friends and hold them close to your heart, the memories will inspire you over time, as you are on the right path towards love and light.

The magic of the light within

Look within for the light that shines bright.
Like a sun high in the sky above the clouds.
Rising and setting with each beautiful day.

Others shield their eyes as you shine so bright.
As they get used to your newfound light.
They warm to your light's soft, magic glow.

Let them absorb your warmth and strength.
You are their new teacher and mentor.
Watch their light glow like the stars above.

The magic of the light is within you all.
This divine light never switches off or fades.
Your flame travels with you on all your journeys.

The many journeys you take are lit like a torch.
Your flame grows brighter with knowledge and wisdom.
You are a beacon on a mountaintop, shining out.

Others will be drawn and guided by your light.

You know this and feel the magic of spirit within.

Now sparkle your magic light into your world and beyond.

Do not doubt or hold back and shine bright, my friends.

Heal yourself

The healing you seek starts from within and then reaches up to the divine. The good intent of the healer will channel the love and the touch of God as they rest their hands on you.

Open your heart up to this wonderful healing source so you can feel its strength. This is the strength of the divine that you need to trigger your healing process.

Open your mind and heart to accepting that all will be well, and give over to us any anger, fears, doubt and trust as you will be whole again.

Your mind holds the key to successful healing; you know you block your progress. Imagine yourself well, running free in Mother Nature, pain-free and loved.

With the combination of your freed mind and the healing touch of the divine, you will be released from your health restrictions and be able to live the life you desire.

The silence

The silent being, alone in the shadows, no light shines in their world. You do not see them; they are hidden behind closed doors, shadows of their former selves.

They are seen as loners and ignored by their fellow humanity, look; you can see the sadness in their eyes. Was this isolation living by choice? Some would say yes as it's easier to believe that.

We would say my friends your paths are for love and companion ship with a loving hand reaching out to you in the darkness. Open the closed doors and don't be afraid to step into the shadows.

You can bring love and light to the lonely in your world. Stretch out a helping hand to those living in a silent existence. That loving touch will bring them forward into the light out of the shadows and chatter of companionship.

Gather near

Hold out your arms and gather your loved ones near.

They will give you strength my friends.

They are your inspiration, your listeners and your support network.

Their love is your love.

Your light is their light.

Blend and be as one, you will know peace.

A single voice

I have a voice – I am lost in my time
I have a voice – I sit in the silence
I have a voice – I have a tear in my eye
I have a voice – I am in the crowd
I have a voice – I hide in the shadows
I have a voice – I am afraid to speak
I have a voice – Now it is silenced

I am your voice – I will hold your hand
I am your voice – I will bring in the light
I am your voice – I will help you speak
I am your voice – I will be your thoughts
I am your voice – I take away the fear
I am your voice – I will sing with you
I am your voice – I will speak out loud

We are the voice – We hold your hand
We are the voice – We are whole again
We are the voice – We hear all thoughts
We are the voice – We will grow together
We are the voice – We will learn together
We are the voice – We are now one mind

The Dark Shadow Within

Our wish is for your body to be born pure and cleansed surrounded by love. Your body cleansed of any darkness and substances, which your world could harm it by.

There are those mothers nurturing the fetus among humanity that take harmful substances that affect the baby's body and inner spirit. But when these babies are born we try to cleanse them of the substances so their path in life can be clean and wholesome again.

These substances come from your Mother Earth, which could be used for healing if used correctly amongst humanity. But the drug warlords among man still have the greed and hunger for wealth taking these substances and sell them among you to cause harm and darkness in the light. There is no discrimination for them who they sell it to and the humans that get caught up in this drug world.

The human body and mind is so strongly affected by this abuse they inflict on themselves, they see no reasoning and commit acts through desperation to fulfill their addiction. Their acts of great unkindness cause great pain against their fellow human beings. They push their loved ones to the furthest boundaries and put up a wall so they can't get in.

But you must remember my friends that these humans need help; no matter what atrocities they cause through substance abuse they need your help. They need to be bought back from the brink from where their body can no longer be abused any more. To stop the hurt they cause others while on this path and to bring them back from the loneliness they feel within.

Their inner spirit does not have the strength to fight this type of abuse my friends even with our help. We see their loved ones do everything they can to try and bring their loved ones back from the brink of despair. But the substances and the dark shadows in the world that push these drugs for wealth, outweigh the single factor of the love of the loved ones.

Once the human has taken drugs they are easy targets and dragged back in to that life of despair again. Their mind has been weakened and they look for a way to forget the dark shadow within them.

We see this is a massive problem all over your world and causes us great sadness. We see the individual who think their lives are unhappy, or are mentally not coping, seeking a release from these feelings, which at the start the substance they chose gives them. It gives them the kick to make them smile and feel good again and this is how it all starts my friends, the spiral of the drugs, alcohol and despair for that single human and all that love them.

If only these humans could stand back at those moments in their life's and look at the good things in their life's, if only we could lift that despair from their minds so they don't go down that path. This is not a chosen path my friends for any of you, it is a challenge we see that faces us among you all.

We see the human character can be weak and is influenced by other humans that take you down this path, the weak are targeted by the substance suppliers, who themselves are not users. Remember my friends if you see a child or adult you think is abusing a substance in your lives try to intervene, try to be strong, try and help them. You will hit walls, you will hit barriers but you are the stronger because you are not on the substances that will block your mind and your physical body to the love and light and the divine love that is out there.

These people need your help and not to be shunned, you will not get any thanks back from them my friends, apart from the hope that one day they will live a clean life again. This is part of your ascension, you will give so much and not receive any thing back my friends. The reward will be seeing that human is who they once were and not what they had become.

The truth

The lies you spin divide your soul, as you sink deeper and deeper into despair.

The harm you cause split the love of the unity of family and friends.

The spiraling guilt sits within you and repair seems beyond reach.

Remember all can be healed my friend when the truth is spoken.

The forgiving nature of others will allow you heal your broken soul.

With the truth you will become one again with yourself and the universe.

Today is a new day, my friends.

Push forward with your lives and step away from the dark into the light.

Every day is a fresh start for you all to wipe the slate clean.

Cleanse your soul of any negativity and bring in only positive light.

Treasure those close to your hearts and let their love in.

Surround yourself with only love, then this lets you love in return.

Life is a gift, my friends, unwrap it and live it to the full.

The infinity of creation

The thread of your existence is spread across all creation

Infinity lies beyond your conscious mind, limited by your thoughts.

Your soul within holds the consciousness of this knowledge you need.

Every cell in your body holds the ancient frequency of ethical existence.

Be true to your original source of creation to find this knowledge.

Infinity is a word that holds no boundaries of existence in your mind.

Let go of your restrictive mindsets to find the answers of creation.

My covid cocoon

For nearly a year I have been cocooned in space and time, reflecting on how my life used to be when I was free.

My cocoon has kept me warm and safe from the fear, just popping out now and then to see the world out there.

I saw a glimpse of tired faces hidden behind doors and masks, I rushed a round so I could quickly finish my weekly tasks.

My cocoon locked out the predators and dictators of life, allowing me to evolve far away from the world's strife.

My cocoon was generous in nature allowing me walks alone, taking time for reflection for the life's that have returned home.

My cocoon was a place of prayer and healing for the world, always trusting all will be well knowing we just need to be bold.

The day arrived when hope was felt across our Mother Earth, nervously I left my safe space to adventure out keeping the faith.

I faced the healers of our world as they gave nectar of new life, seeing others leaving their cocoons, sister, brother, husband, and wife.

As we waited in the ques of time a light shone down from above, a light of comfort, oneness, and hope for all giving us boundless love.

As I slowly emerge from my cocoon, I feel so spiritually different now, I see the universe with new eyes and discovered things I never knew.

As you emerge have faith and trust as you experience this new earth, hold each other by the hand as we move forward in this time of faith.

Your cocoon has changed you into a beautiful being of self-worth, Now fly high and be the best you can be on this new beautiful earth.

Time is a healer

We send healing to your heart, as time will fade the pain and wishing for when you are left with only the pure love and memories.

The love causes the pain, believe us there is no shame as your empty heart aches and the hole you feel, will fill back up with the unconditional love you once held.

Take your time to drink the divine love to heal your soul and remember they live on in a reality of love, always a touch away.

Trust you will embrace each other again living on in the highest heavenly realms.

Grief

Grief is one of the rawest emotions as a human you will ever experience. Grief takes your energies down into to the lowest depths of despair.

Grief comes from experiencing true love in your human lives. The unconditional love of a parent, lover, friend or animal owner.

Unconditional love is the purest highest energy a human will ever experience. The pure love energy can heal all and take away the despair of grief.

When the physical form of which you love stops living, remember the love you had for them. Remember the joy they bought in to your life.

Remember the happiest moment, the laughter and the kindness you shared. Forgive the moments of anger, frustration and hardship you faced together.

The memory of that life that has now ended will always be in your heart. Their ever-lasting love will always be in your mind, body and your soul.

Remember in separation your loved one walks beside you holding your hand. Your loved one will always shower love down upon you trying to ease your pain.

Your loved ones want you to smile, sing and dance again in your lifetime. They will smile, sing and dance with you as you find the joy in life again.

So my friends lift your grieving heart towards heaven and feel the touch of pure love. Feel the unconditional love of your loved ones who are just a thought and touch away.

Your thoughts and the love from your heart and soul will draw them near. If you sit and listen and feel you will sense their touch of love all around.

Love heals the wounds of time, remember the love and you will smile and find the joy in your hearts again.

Always in my heart

As your heart lays broken in pieces with their last breath.

They hold you in their heart for comfort for the journey ahead.

They are grateful for their time with you on this Mother Earth.

They hold on to the memories gathered from their birth.

The unconditional love they gave was to hold you in the divine grace.

This love will never die and is held in the memory of their face.

They ask you to step back and remember all the fun times you had.

Reflect on the love you hold in your own heart, so you are not sad.

They want you to be happy and to share all your love again.

Remember the years you spend with a pet is never in vain.

Embrace this knowledge given to you so you have time to heal.

They know you pain inside and everything you feel is real.

They stay by your side to you meet again when it is Gods will.

Trust the journey of grief as it's from the unconditional love you feel.

Section 4

Enlighten

So stay in the sunshine, smile out to the world, radiating your inner happiness and you will change all of those that see your spark of love and light.

Tide of time

Time slips over you like a wave;
let it wash away your fears.

Let it gently soothe your soul
and wipe away your tears.

Feel the gentle ripples on your skin,
feel our touch on your face.

All will resolve in time dear friend just
take life at a timely pace.

As you drift on the tide of time,
you will feel our love and kiss.

We will take away your pain;
your heart will burst with bliss.

So my friends have faith in us,
give over your heart to our light.

You will now shine in the world;
your love has won the fight.

Nurture your soul

Nurturing your souls is key to you travelling towards a life of light and love. Kindness, compassion, and empathy are just a few things that nurture the soul. Giving out love and receiving love back into your lives is also a key factor. Live in the positive energy Mother Earth gives you, lifting your vibrations towards us.

All these will ignite your soul and your mind's thinking. Don't be afraid to speak out your thoughts, passions and creative ideas.

Think out of the box, my friends, and share these thoughts with the world. Do not let fellow humanity hold you back.

Now ignite your soul and shine into the dark parts of your world, bringing love and light.

Carry our torch

Your heart is whole when linked with the soul.

Your mind is strong when calm and still.

Your energy vibrates when connected to us.

Your vibrations ripple out across the ethos.

We feel your heartbeat within our spirit.

We hear your mind's thoughts with ours.

We feel your vibration across our realm.

We touch your hand so you stay calm.

As we blend, our energies entwine.

Our love and light becomes your candle.

Our flame becomes your journey's path.

The candle will flicker but we will guide you.

You are our ambassadors, so carry our torch.

You take our messages across your time.

You will vibrate out our love into the world.

We are all one; be strong, trust and shine, my friends.

Turn Dark into light

If you are feeling your days are dark

Pause…

Light a candle and make a wish

Listen…

We are all around you to give you strength

Feel…

Ask for a sign from us to be near

See…

It might be an angel feather

Touch…

We will touch your heart and inspire you

You…

You are loved and precious to us

Light…

Light your candle and shine into your world

Love…

Love is all around you love yourself.

Be happy, positive and true

Do not hurt those near to your heart,
look at your actions and theirs.

Do not judge too quickly;
look at them as a whole.

If you cannot be together,
pull apart, but keep them in your heart.

Rise above the hurt and forgive,
life is for living and being happy.

True love is smiles and happiness,
being together even from a distance.

Help, guide and support each other,
do no tear each other down.

Only you can evaluate your life.
Do you smile, and laugh together?

Trust and have faith in each other,
hold this in your heart and love life.

Look in the deepest part of your soul,
their lie the answers and the way forward.

Be happy, positive and true.

The spirit from within

Your human spirit joins with your divine spirit,
both working together to create a unique being.

You link at the moment of conceptions innocence,
a spark of the divine pure in love and light.

You both work tirelessly together to fulfill your life's path;
you all have a mission and a message to be sent out to others.

The separation of your spirits is planned when you return home; the physical presence is then missed by your loved ones left behind.

They also miss your heavenly spirit, as this was your soul, the essence of you, and your true self that shone out to others.

There is great joy when you all reunite in the divine home source, the source of love and light, true knowing and knowledge.

You will wrap your love around each other again my friends when you all meet to carry on your spirit paths together.

Connect

Your higher self is waiting in pure love existence,
don't let your Earth self let you down.

Smile as you have never smiled before in the mirror,
then look at your reflection beaming back at you.

This is how others will see you; when you smile, a beam
of light shines in their world.

Light up the world

Light up the world with your smile.

This will reflect in others like a mirror.

Smiling and laughter is contagious,
be the person that spreads it; all will smile with you.

Smile and laugh your way through life.

Connection from within

Take your mind and look within. What do you see?

Do you see the mist of times gone by lying within?

Do you see sunbeams breaking through the clouds?

Do you see a beautiful existence of love and light?

Do you see shadows and flickers of distant hope?

Do you see doubt and a lost spirit within?

To find what lies within your inner being, you need to sit in the silence, my friends and focus on your inner essence and spirit. Your spirit carries its history for all of you to rediscover while on this Earth plane. When you connect truly to this inner being that lives within, all the shadows, doubts and mistrust will be forgotten. The light will shine in, bouncing you forward on your true path to find kindness, love and the faith of the divine.

Remember, as you connect to your inner being, we are all here celebrating with you, only a touch away for guidance and the love you need while on this exciting journey on Earth.

My friends, celebrate your wonderful journey with spirit, and take this out to the world, teach and inspire so others can connect with the spirit being that lies within them.

The twist of time

The twist of time as it spins like a star in the sky; it falls and unwinds like a tight coil coming down with the divine.

It touches you within your heart, within your spirit and as you unwind and spin with time you find you are renewed.

Your path lies on a tunnel of divine love, turning and twisting through the universe as it heads towards us, and as you follow this journey within, you will find your beginning.

The clocks are turning, the time is twisting, it bends back and forth, and you are flexible with this within your spirit - you know it's worth.

Follow the twists and bends of time, to find your hope, love and the divine.

Your faith will bring you back to us, back to the place of love.

New Horizons

While on your life's journey on earth and in the spirit realm, there will be opportunities placed in your path. Look at these opportunities as improving yourselves, my friends, improving your skills, your mental mind, physical body and your being as a whole.

Don't be afraid to go towards a new horizon that is shining before you like a beacon of light. As you reach that horizon, don't be afraid of the next horizon, as there will be many through your life's path.

Many of you wait for the sun to rise and fall again before you make decisions; sometimes decisions need to be made quicker, so you do not miss the opportunities that are placed before you.

When you start to awaken to the spirit realm and see the sun shining brightly and the stars in the heavens, and we come knocking on your door. The spirit realm places new opportunities and signs near and far on your horizon.

As you connect with us you will gain confidence; the new horizons will never be a problem for you, you will always reach them. The new opportunities you set yourself and we set before you, will not be a challenge to you they will be an adventure, my friends. They will be an adventure to help you complete your whole self while here on Earth.

So take these opportunities, do not have fear, only trust and trust that you are sailing towards the right horizon.

The journey of knowledge

A jump   A skip   A step

How are you moving forward with the next stage of your journey on Earth?

A stride   A leap   A climb

Do you have the faith and trust to take the next step?

A look   A glance   A smile

Observe all around you so you can make the positive choices you need to take for the next part of your journey on your life's path.

Listen   Trust   Faith

You have your spirit friends to guide you and all the answers you seek lay within you.

Connect   Love   Give

Go forward without hesitation and follow your life's path to the light.

Divine   God   Universe

The answers you seek are in reach, look, listen and observe, it is all within your grasp.

Enjoy   Blessed   Home

Now sit back and enjoy the ride on Earth knowing you are protected until you return back to us.

Teaching   Inspired   Learn

Your journey of gaining knowledge will carry on in the spirit realm and you are always learning and ascending to the light of the divine.

Spirit   Angel   Heaven

The love of the divine awaits you, stay safe in the knowledge you are loved and guided back to us to take the next steps on your spirit journey.

Abundance

Abundance comes from within; it is your kindness, love and true self.

Abundance is your family, friends and animals in your life.

Abundance is being safe, warm and nourished.

Abundance is security, health and shelter.

Abundance is you as a whole and all the goodness around you.

When you have abundance give it out to those that don't.

Live in love and light and you will have abundance.

The Reflection

Look through the mirror to the horizon beyond.
Is this the true reflection of what you feel?
Does this mirror reflect the true you?
Feel your emotions being reflected back to you.
Do you recognise the emotions you now see?
Now reflect these feelings back to us.
They now belong to us in the mirror.

Look through the mirror to the horizon beyond.
What do you see? It should be clear.
The sun is shining back at you now.
The mirror now reflects the true you.
We are always there looking back at you.
We wait for your questions and answers.
We reflect healing out to your soul.

Look through the mirror to the horizon beyond.
Do you see the clear road ahead?
Your reflection now blends with the sunset.
Do not stop looking ahead as the horizon never ends.

As you travel forward we walk beside you.

Trust in the reflection you now see.

You are now whole and we are all as one.

Twilight years

As you reach your twilight years it is a time for human reflection.

You reflect on the pain in your life

You reflect on the shame in your life

You reflect on the anger in your life

You reflect on the moments you missed

You reflect on the moments of doubt

You reflect on the love of a child lost

You reflect on lost love

You reflect on times of happiness

You reflect on what might have been

You reflect on life as a dream

But remember my friends this is all experiences of the human race. There should never be any thought of what if… I should have done this… if only…

What came about in your life was meant to be as it has been a pathway of learning and gaining knowledge.

As your twilight years end and you pass over to your new life in the stars with us, you will understand the journey that you took while on this Earth plane.

The Journey is for ascension, for a better way of being for humanity and for spirit self.

If you wish my friend when you have reflected on your life on Earth you may come back again and try to better the life you had before.

Or take the time to reflect further and try something new to enhance your growth while you are back with us in the spirit realm.

The six sense

When we say beauty is in the eye of the beholder, it is not just the physical body it is the soul that shines the beauty as well. You use all your five senses to make these conclusions that influence your decisions.

When you master seeing, smell, taste, listening and touch you can then master the sixth sense *all-knowing*. You cannot see this six sense it is linked with your human flesh, soul, higher self and the divine unconditional love.

The eye sees the beauty of the flesh.
The eye sees the beauty of the world.
The eye sees the beauty of the soul.

The nose filters the air you breathe.
The nose smells the scent of Mother Earth
The nose scents fear and death.

The mouth allows us to flourish.
The mouth allows our spoken voice.
The mouth is a warning sign of survival.

The ear hears the world around you.
The ear is a link to all humanity.
The ear is a tuned to your inner soul.

Touch is your first awareness of your world.
Touch is the kiss of the divine.
Touch is knowing you are loved.

All knowing is the intuition of the soul.

All knowing is living out of the box you know.
All knowing is being as one in unconditional love.

You can reach all knowing state by enhancing your mind through meditation and mindfulness. Dedication to this and looking after your physical body is key to achieving the full use of the six sense. This has always been with you; you just need to retrigger it.

The breath of the wind

The journey of life moves along on the breathe of the wind. Leaves will tumble down before you on your path.

The question is my friends do you kick them away? OR do you stand, observe, admire and hold this gift from nature?

To stand and observe what's around you can become quiet space. You will recharge and set your minds thoughts on the right path.

Please watch where you tread in life like footprints in the sand. Once past, the sea will wash them away, the moment is gone.

Don't look back my friends always forward on your paths. Watch for the beauty of what we set before you, signs from nature.

The choice is always yours where you tread and the path you take. Take that moment in time to hold that autumn leaf and be still.

Love and be loved

You are here to fulfil a role while on earth; you could be a teacher, shop assistant, father, mother, auntie, friend, doctor, scientist, explorer, leader, inspirer – these are just a few of them.

BUT your real purpose is to love and be loved, united in peace and living as one.

To help this, start by taking away the words *they, them* and *others,* and live in a single clarity of oneness.

The bubble burst

As the world changes around you, your bubble of trust burst, shattering your dreams.

When you feel your dreams are broken into pieces, trust it's time for new beginnings.

Dreams are missions to be completed and these can change on your Earth life's path.

Sometimes the world needs to be shaken and awoken to a better reality for humanity.

The burst bubble tests you all, creating a new reality for new dreams and future doors to open.

As you step into this new frequency of love on Earth, take time to reset those dreams.

Dreams come from the soul that is your life's Satnav revealing the map of direction.

Trust the inner intuition to create a new bubble in the new reality of your world.

The Bubble

I feel like I am in a bubble floating around out of time.
I feel safe in my bubble as I watch others float by.
I see rainbows and hearts painted in the sky.
I hear laughter and song in the wind chimes up high.

I'm not sure when I entered my bubble of peace.
I am now free flowing out of the race of life.
I am floating above the fear and panic of earth.
I am sure we are waiting for the new birth.

In my peace I see nature running free with no fear.
I see clear oceans and pure air and a new creation.
I know the spirit of the universe sings to us now.
We are learning what the ancients always knew.

They are saying to me my bubble must burst.
I must return to the new Mother Earth.
I take a breath as I take up my path of life.
I am back here wondering what to do next.

I wonder the streets and listen to the silence.
Everywhere I look is empty of human form.
Nature has a voice again that is loud and clear.

I feel different this time, as I have no fear.

The normality I knew before has gone away.
I now live a new life where no one must pay.
We are healed from within laughing in the wind.
We are all now as one as from time began.

I am grateful for the lessons that I have been taught.
I now tell our story to the children of our world.
They now live in the peace of the bubble floating free.
Our children know only love as they smile at me.

I now know I still have much to give on this earth.
I walk my path in new grace, kindness, and love.
I will inspire and teach the awakened ones.
We will now all unite as one for the good of man.

The awakening of a new age is what I have seen.
Knowing that some suffered but all were loved.
I now move forward with trust in my heart.
Trusting my life journey to the day I depart.

Section 5

From the stars

The Universe is yours, go out into the endless space and search for the wisdom and knowledge you seek.

A message from the old gods

Our race spread across the universe, finding grace amongst the stars. Our supremacy conquered your world and you saw us as gods. Humanity worshipped the paths we walked on, but our time with you was short.

We aligned our structures with the heavens above and we left you our signs. Now draw the map to find the inner message and as you trace the lines of your time, our story will unfold.

We left humanity with our plan as the last of us faded to dust. Our memories sit within your DNA and the hidden depth of your oceans. You now await our return with inner hope of change for mankind.

Our home world waits our second contact with humanity when you are ready to receive us. We wait for you all to embrace unconditional love to aid your ascension, which will bring the moment of pure clarity needed to hear our message and be seen.

Only then will our journey begin again to help humanity.

Love and blessings to all.

We wait

We wait shielded from view, standing shoulder to shoulder with you all. We are a touch away, as we watch over you.

We visit you in dreams, stepping into your visions and are often seen. We leave messages and give healing as you peacefully dream.

We wait for you to connect to us, so you can recognise your mission while here on Earth. We are patient, kind and have unconditional love for you all as we wait.

We ask you to open your eyes and hearts to us, then we will come into view. We wait in our star ship and for Earth to wake up and ascend to the stars above and beyond.

Love and blessings to all.

The third dimension matrix

The matrix holds the fear within, never fading from view. Hold on tight as you breakdown the walls and resonate with the new vibration that has held you all in place for so long.

It's time to break free of your restrictive chains that bound you to fear. Break away and the walls will crumble letting in the love and light you all need.

As you break free there will no longer be any doubt. You will change beyond recognition and smiling with the love from humanity.

The matrix will never return to the old dark frequency and as the new light shines in humanity will ascend in to unconditional love for all.

You will shine into the universe and take your rightful place with us amongst the stars.

Your destiny waits.

The Moment

The sparkles among the many stars, sits within your hearts and souls.

We wait for you to shine bright trusting the pathway to find the light.

Acceptance of ascension beings beyond the knowledge of your mind.

You will finely understand the universe and the mysteries of Earth and time.

We come to you in your dreams, as we wait beyond the horizons.

As we filter into your human minds, the first contact has been spoken.

We will become part of your day and in your mindful thoughts at night.

So when that moment of first physical contact is made, the humans of your world are no longer afraid.

Your future will be set bright as the shining stars in the dark night.

Look for messages from the stars

Reach for the stars

Reach for the top of the highest mountain

Reach for the top of the highest trees

Reach beyond your wildest dreams

Reach into your heart for strength

Reach to your higher self for guidance

Never look down, never look back

Just reach for your dreams, they are within your grasp.

Cosmic reality

The cosmic reality of the mind is not beyond your reach.

The stars are the pathway to the unknown that you seek.

The galaxies are the steering wheels of knowledge on your path.

They guide you beyond your perceived reality from all that's past.

The universe has a future story to tell all that chooses to listen.

The pages are there to be turned to bring you to a higher existence.

Look beyond what your mind can see to hear and feel our reality.

We are just a thought away waiting for you to connect this day.

The ancient healing ways return

We have started the process of healing humanity, but we need your help.

Many of you are becoming aware of the ancient knowledge of life.

This knowledge sits within your DNA and deep conscious minds.

We are guiding the knowledge of LIGHT to the darkness that lives within the shadows of your time.

Be aware of the sparks of recognition you will feel as you walk in the shadows of your reality.

Deja vu will become the norm as you start to recognise the old ancient healing ways of humanity.

Embrace this time on your earth and become a leader of ancient knowledge and teach these old ways to your children.

The alliance

Many off world beings have joined the earth to form an alliance.

We come from many sources of creation in the universe to aid humanity.

We bring you a wealth of knowledge to bring humanity new thought processes.

Our mission is to change your perception of your world.

To bring clarity of minds so you can see beyond your restrictive mind process of thought.

You will find us in your minds through telepathic thought, meditations, and dreams.

We wait for humanity to clear their minds of hate, doubt and work in the unison of love.

When your perceptions have altered, we will walk among you as allies and friends.

Join us in this alliance and accept our hands of friendship.

One day at a time

As we watch humanity charge through your life's – we see you miss so much of your world.

Mother Earth still has so much beauty to share with you that has not been destroyed by humanity.

We see humans still have much love in their hearts to share with each other.

But the speed of your reality you are creating is not letting you see or feel this in your everyday life's.

Step back and take life at a slower pace not worrying about your past or future, but your present moment you are living in.

Live one day at a time, this will help you see your world in a new perspective.

It will bring you appreciation for all there is and what you have in your life's.

This in return will ignite within you the changes you need to alter your world for the good of all and help you work in unison to heal Mother Earth.

Section 6

Find your true self

*Your path will find the right words for your voice.
You will find the right voice for your path*

Your voice

Your path will find the right words for your voice.

You will find the right voice for your path.

The vibration is from the soul; the tone is from your heart.

Pitch this right and we hear, answering you in a chorus of song.

Hear our voices, loved ones, as we hear yours.

All will be clear and true to you.

Time is the healer

To be whole is to be honest with yourself.
Time distorts memories and trust.
The memory left is not what truly was.

To trust is based on true self-worth.
Move on forward and do not look back.
Your memories are left back in time.

Your past will always be there with you.
Bring forward the love, not the hurt.
Time is your healer; just trust in us.

Time holds old stories, move forward to
write your future story, and don't relive the pages.

You are awesome

You are you

You let your light shine

You are strong

You are wise

You will learn from hurt

You will heal from harm

You know who you are

You need to be you

You are awesome

Shine

Your world showers sadness down on you
that humanity has made and reflects out to you.

Your soul will cry with others' pain and sorrow;
you will shed and wipe away a silent tear too.

Release this pain from your hearts so you can see
the light on your path to travel your journeys.

Yes listen, feel and then send healing wishes to the
suffering and souls that have gone home.

Surround yourself with our love's protection and
live your lives shining your love out to humanity.

A heavenly shield surrounds you to protect you,
we wish you to shine, my friends and be you.

Be your true self

Confirmation of who you are is deep within you.

Find yourself to find the confirmation you seek.

To be you, be happy and follow your passions in life.

Move away from harm and those that do not love you.

You will then find yourself and all the confirmation you need.

Stay in the sunshine

As you rise up out of the darkness into the sunshine my friend, you are blossoming like a pure white lily flower.

Your smile is lighting up many faces and affecting many hearts, don't let your smile ever fade.

As you stride forward with newfound confidence in life and love in your heart, you will find your path.

Your inner beauty is your soul and essence of the divine; a spark of goodness is what you will find inside your soul.

You know the answers, my friend; we are all here with you, guiding, supporting, loving and smiling as you progress.

So stay in the sunshine, smile out to the world, radiating your inner happiness and you will change all of those that see your spark of love and light.

Blessings my friend, walk your path with trust and love.

True self

Your true self lies within you, what's on the
surface can be a false exterior.

Remember that when you judge people
not all is revealed and as it seems.

To know their true self, dig below the surface,
there will be resistance from past fear & hurt.

Don't judge your fellow man and woman,
always look within and find their true light.

Every human has this torch of love and light,
it just gets lost through fear of the unknown.

Don't judge help them shine their light, you will
find their true value in time.

Best friends

The physical form holds the strength of Mother Earth, made up from the elements of life itself.

The physical body holds the source of the divine pure love from beyond, your shell of energy wrapping itself like a cocoon around your spirit friend within.

Your spirit friend lies protected in your human form, connecting to all of you from within and beyond.

Joy is beheld as you travel your journey together on Mother Earth. You are like best friends on an adventure to bringing love and kindness and a higher way of being to the Earth plane.

There is no sadness on the day these friends separate forever, only joy is found. The physical form has served its purpose and Mother Earth accepts you back into her bosom.

Your spiritual friend, YOU, travels back home to pick up on your spirit life you had before your Earth journey. Your physical life is never forgotten, the human essence living on in your spirit with the knowledge and wisdom gained while here on Earth.

Remember, forever blessed, forever wiser and loved beyond words at all times – while joined together and separated at death of the physical form, your light will always shine.

Finding Harmony

Harmony lies within you like a flower bud waiting to open, it waits to be released on your Earth life's path. When the flower blooms the pollen is released and will swirl round you, cocooning and protecting you from the fears and the doubts you have about yourself and the world around you.

Harmony is a friend; it protects you from the unknown; when found it sets you on the track of life; remember you are born with harmony within from the moment you take your first breath.

To sustain the harmony you crave, my friends, you need to look at your life, the balance of love against fear, trust against doubt and to manifest what you desire in your life through positive thought.

Harmony can be achieved, my friends, take the simple moment when you watch a bee buzzing above a flower to collect pollen, imagine the wings slow down and you see the bee in a moment of time held in suspension, this is a perfect moment of harmony.

Harmony is when you feel peace and calmness within, a happiness that can never fade. This sits within you all my friends; it is only a touch away. Spirit is harmony, we live in harmony, in love and trust, and this can all be yours.

Some of you see this as out of reach, beyond far horizons; you might see this as a challenge to achieve in the turmoil of your life. But if you could just sit and take your time, and the moments needed sitting listening to the world around by tuning into Mother Nature, the spirit realm and beyond, then you will start to find that balance within, my friends.

Once you have that balance within you, it will trigger the harmony you seek. The harmony of a calm mind that does not judge others, does not criticize, that accepts what comes and trusts that all will be good and well. The harmony of the body, health, the nourishment balance of food and water, this is all vital to creating the harmony you need, my friends.

Once you find the harmony within, the turmoil, the friction, the doubts, the non-believers, the ridiculers will sit at your boundary, they will no longer affect you or hurt you, they will exist with you and be part of your lives, but they cannot harm you. You have found the harmony we create, the protection you need to carry on with your spiritual journey.

As you progress on this journey you are taking, my friends, the harmony you have now found will be seen by others; there will be jealousy, as we have said, people will recoil from you, but then others will be drawn to you. This is all part of your journey, your journey of finding harmony within you.

The key thing for you is when you find this harmony and acceptance of who you are and the balance of health and life, you will be able to reflect this out to others, it will become part of your teachings, part of your way of being. You will find others will wish to be as you are, living in harmony. Everything you have learnt in this life has come to this stage of your journey and will be what you can teach to others, the good and the bad of your experiences and how to balance themselves. Tell others how you felt when you first experienced spirit, tell your stories, my friends, you will be surprised how people will want to listen to you. They will want to hear your wisdom and philosophy to balance their lives, as they are seeking harmony themselves. They will not realise this at first, but their inner spirit knows this and is trying to encourage them with their higher self in the spirit realm to seek this harmony.

So reflect and realise that just one simple word from you can change someone's life. As you reflect your harmony out to others you will become more balanced, more rested within yourself, and you will be in the harmony state that you need to walk your path in life, my friends.

Live in beautiful harmony, rested, peaceful and trusting and with the divine light within you, and you will have wonderful lives.

Intuition

Hesitation causes uncertainty, uncertainty affects your confidence, and lack of confidence affects your self-esteem.

Don't hesitate in life, have confidence and follow your intuition, it is a good friend to you; believe in and trust it, as it is a gift that comes from us.

The twin higher self

Death brings a new altered dimensional state of being. The gravity your physical body lived in fades away. The heaviness that restricted your lighter self is gone as you are released.

You are now between the two worlds in a floating dream state. You can see the old world and are drawn to the new light beyond. The light is so full of love and vibrancy you are drawn to it.

You now move forward not wishing to look back. This is so familiar to you as your ethereal body goes towards the light. There are others now traveling with you, all with a common goal.

The feeling of coming home now surrounds you. The light draws you on then you see a being coming towards you. They are so familiar it's like looking at an identical twin of yourself.

You join hands and become one reunited in unconditional love. You move forward to be greeted by familiar beings. There is so much to say and show your old friends.

Your story will be told and healing will be given. You are now ready to continue your life in the light. Now will you stay or be reborn back to the world you left or a new world? This is up to you my friend.

Age gracefully

Do not be afraid of the human condition called age. The body is a shell for you to live in until you return to us.

You do not age on the Earth plane you are one with your higher self. Also remember age gives grace and wisdom which is to be given to others.

Embrace the Earth years and enjoy all they have to offer you. These experiences will help you evolve in your spiritual journey.

Remember you reflect out to others what you are inside. Stay young at heart and keep the beauty within you shining at all times.

Now sit back and enjoy the ride on Mother Earth. Be true to yourself and embrace the human form.

The soul has eyes

Look at others as you would wish them to look upon you, their eyes will always tell the truth.

Always be true to yourself and others; see them through their eyes, deep into their souls, then trust your intuition.

Time is the essence of your existence, look beyond time to find your true self.

Have a vision

Your vision
is our vision,
live it,
breath it,
we will be part of it.

True love

Today is the day you are going to find TRUE LOVE.

The person who is going to love you in this way, is not your soul mate, your dog or friend, it is YOU.

Look within yourself and there lies the purest love of all, the unconditional love of the divine.

When you connect with this inner love which is YOU, you will learn to love who you are.

Acceptance of self is the connection and doorway to true love of the heart, soul and beyond.

Once you love yourself with true love then all will be clear, and you will move forward in life with love always in your heart.

Remember the experiences of love in your life will never be as pure as yourself love and connection to the divine.

When you achieve this, it will attract the truest love intentions from others and you will understand the love connection that's sits within your heart beat.

Reflection of self

Today I woke up wishing my self-happy birthday
I felt the same old me that I was at thirty three
Young, lively, and very hopeful of the life to be
I sat on the bed reflecting on the years gone by

As I crossed the room, I caught a reflection of my self
I stopped, as I felt confused by what I could see
This woman before me I did not truly recognise
Who was this older lady that stared back at me?

A voice said 'but this is you my dear friend'
You have lived sixty years on this beautiful land
Look deep into the mirror as you are there
Look into your eyes to see your soul without fear

I stood and watched my reflection and yes, I could see
There were two reflections staring back at me
My younger self smiling reaching out a guiding hand
Then my older me, a friend full of wisdom and love

I realised we are as one, intertwined in the earth life
This younger inner self I know is my lifelong friend
We have been on a journey together of learning on earth
Together we are whom I understand to be me

I realised the aging shell and younger self is who I am
We work together as a team to be as one on the path of life
So we laughed out loud and sang each other a song
Happy birthday to us and happy to be united as one.

Section 7

Messages from the angels

*As we wrap our wings of love around you,
know you are always safe and loved by the angels.*

Angel love

As you wrap your arms around the one you love,
the angels wrap their love around you.

We are the safe, warm feeling of love and security,
the safety net of life for when you tumble.

We are here to guide and help you on your path;
ask and we will be there with you.

Have no doubt or fear as we are near, call out and
we will answer your wishes.

Look for the answers around you in everyday life,
feel our love and strength as we walk beside you.

As we wrap our wings of love around you,
know you are always safe and loved by the angels.

Angels by my side

I have no enemies.

I cannot hate.

I do believe in fate.

I have only known friends.

Some turned bad.

Some drifted away.

Some stayed by my side.

The memories help me grow.

The hurt gave me strength.

I hold on to the love.

I let go of the pain.

I walk my path with pride.

With angels by my side.

I no longer fear the unknown.

I will love my life until I return home.

Touched by an earth angel

Frightened, lonely, holding in the pain,
waiting for the day freedom is gained.

Longing for a spirit of your kind, to
stop and gently touch you with love.

The days of endless grind, lack of
the divine sits inside your mind.

You rock to and fro with hopelessness,
wondering when the pain will go.

You hear a gentle footstep beside you;
a hand rests on you, the touch of an angel.

Peace is within your grasp; a further journey
lies ahead before freedom is found.

The sun drops, there are new smells and
gentle spirits on this new path.

At sunrise your life of chains fades away
and your freedom has been gained.

You now have bliss within your heart,
touched by love and kindness of others.

You have been touched by earth angels
and now walk amongst the green grass.

No more tears, just a smile and the new spirits of your kind in your heart.

Song of the Divine

Listen to the music my friends, the beat of the song. The notes of life that flow along the rhythm of time. The message that is in the words connects with your heart.

Listen to the music of nature, the tune on the wings in flight. The melody of the grasses swaying in the summer breeze. The chorus of notes with the rising dawn on the horizon.

Listen to your angel's song, of love and the divine. The soft enchanting tunes of the melody of the heavens above. Let them resonate through your inner spirit and beyond.

All music is from love my friends and comes from a higher source. Your heart and spirit sings when it connects with a tune of love. Live on that wave of divine music and sing out your love to the world.

An angel knocked on my door today

An angel knocked on my door today.

He said he had come to stay.

He came to play and bring me luck.

He made me laugh and forget my woes.

He bought the sunshine on a cloudy day.

He is my strength and guiding hand.

He is the answer to my prayers.

An angel came into my life to stay today.

He has many angel friends knocking on doors.

When an angel knocks on your door let them in.

They bring the change you have been wishing for.

The day you open the door your journey starts.

So don't be afraid to let the angel in your heart.

At that moment the true healing will begin.

An angel is going to knock on your door today.

Just a pause

As you cross over to the spiritual plane we will lay you to rest.

We will now wait for the many firsts without you in our lives.

Future birthdays, weddings, and births you will always be in our thoughts.

We will look up at the door to see if you are standing there looking back.

We will shed a silent tear at the empty chair waiting to welcome you.

As I cross over to the spiritual plane I send you all my love.

I will wait for the many firsts I will have without you in your lives.

Future birthdays, weddings, and births I will only be a thought away.

Please look up at the door and trust I am looking back at you.

I will wipe away your tears and join you all in the laughter.

Trust we will never be separated in death, it is just a pause.

I rejoined my spiritual journey in heaven living a full life.

I walk beside you on the physical plane of life holding your hand.

Our hearts and souls are connected to we meet again.

Now live your lives to the full knowing I am a touch away.

The Christmas Gift

As Christmas approaches you see no light, the Christmas star is not so bright.

You are rushing around, wondering where the Christmas joy is to be found.

Your thoughts are with the past and present, missing the loved ones that have been Heaven Sent.

You wonder what the future will hold, and when your heart will feel whole.

The Christmas future is bright within you and the light will shine again.

The love you held for loved ones passed sits within the heavenly feast.

They await for your Christmas table to be laid, and family to gather in the joy of the day.

They will come in their turn to give you the wishes and hugs you yearn.

Watch out for the Christmas tingles and the soft brushed kiss sensation on the cheek, these are gifts from your loved ones in the heavenly seat.

Do not mourn us – we still shine bright like the star on Christmas night.

We twinkle like your tree lights do, shining brightly out

to you.

We are the message in your Christmas cracker, bringing joy and laughter.

We are the loved ones forever after.

So hold a candle up to us, my friends, and wish us well in our heavenly realm, for we wish you well on earth too, as you celebrate a Christmas new.

Have a magical Happy New Year

Happy New Year to one and all may your New Year start with some fun.

Don't look back my friend's look forward with TRUST.

Don't look back my friend's look forward with LOVE.

Tread your journey in the light as you were born to live with love, kindness and honesty.

Believe in yourself and believe in us and you will not waver from your life's path.

Do not rush into the New Year because of fear at what you might not achieve.

Take it day-by-day, step-by-step and believe in the magic you can create.

Look into yourself and heal and give over the grief, anger and the pain you hold within.

Leave this with us my friends so you can move on in to a better space.

When you have released this into the universe your New Year will be filled with grace. You will see how it unfolds enveloping you in our heavenly hugs.

We will protect you and move you forward, just trust we are by your side. We are always listening, we hear your thoughts, and we hear your prayers, just trust the answers will appear.

Stay positive in the light, move out of the darkness and the shadows, because you have the right to see the divine and the love that can touch you in this lifetime.

Watch for signs from the heavenly ones, trust they are from us, ask and you will receive.

Never doubt my friends always trust and you will have the most magical New Year xxx

The Angel Hug

As the angels take the one you love from earth boundaries, they travel home to the heavenly realms.

Their physical form is laid to rest celebrating their life at its best.

Don't worry my friend they are safe in our arms, they're journey continues in the heavenly realms.

Let the sadness fall away and remember the happy days.

Place a smile on your face and remember their grace.

They will always stay true to you and the love you knew.

As you travel your path of life and love, remember my friend they are always there giving you that angel hug.

Now let go of the sadness and remember the love and one day you will meet in heaven above.

Earth angel of the streets

I have no home as I walk the city streets all alone.

I feel vulnerable in the cold and dark of the unknown.

I ask for coins but the people's cold eyes turn away.

I am getting desperate now as the days go slowly by.

I now have a choice to sale my body or drugs on the street.

I choose the drugs so I can find warmth at night and eat.

I thought I was safe with my newfound friends.

I was wrong as I am in fear for my life in this drug den.

I chose the street again and moving city to be safe.

There is no choice for me but crime, as I lose my faith.

I am in my darkest hour thinking the world will not miss me.

I am depressed at the bottom of the darkest hole on my knees.

As the rain pours down on me I shiver to the bone.

Then I see an angel in front of me I am no longer a lone.

An earth angel of the street wraps me in her golden light.

She took me to a shelter and said we will make things right.

I am now safe and warm with a newfound self-respect.

I am lucky an earth angel found me that night and showed me love and light.

Heaven's flower

My dear loved one, you will always be within our hearts, as you fly back home with the angels to the gardens of heaven.

You will shine amongst the flowers, the heavenly blue skies, and the pureness and the love of the divine.

We search for your love; we search for your presence to feel your hugs again, knowing that one day we will meet at the heavenly gate.

You are wrapped round our hearts with love, never forgotten, knowing you fly high amongst the angels.

Find your place in the heavenly blooms amongst the stars, so you can shine down on your loved ones.

When we feel low and our hearts grieve, we will look to the sky seeking your smile to release the pain that arises within.

Our Angel

Why the loss of one so young, we hear people say? Why can they not live their life in full until they are old and grey?

Only heaven knows the answers to these questions, my friends, why they have taken one so young back into their angel wings.

Rest in peace, young spirit soul, and we have ease knowing that you are now whole, playing up in the clouds, having fun and running in the heavenly sun.

Our hearts grieve for you, my precious one, but we know a new life for you has just begun. We know not why you had to go home, all we know is you will never be alone.

We miss your physical presence and embrace, but we know you now sit in heaven's grace, and one day when we travel back home we will be reunited in the name of love, never to be broken or separated again.

Our hearts will always be as one, beating the same tune of love from heaven above. So rest in peace in the arms of the angels, my sweet one, and we wait for that day we meet again in heaven's realm.

Rainbow

When you see a rainbow think of me, this is a message of love.

I will slide down to Earth to be with you and hold your hand.

When the rainbow fades, I am the stars that shine brightly down.

Please never frown, smile as I am always around.

Where feathers lie

On the path you tread feathers we lay, to remind you we are here every day.

Remember we are just a thought and breath away and in your heart we will stay.

Section 8

Daily spiritual guidance

*44 messages to help guide you
and others on your daily path in life.*

A divine message to you all

Humanity has drifted over many centuries away from the divine light. The light is not to be feared; it is all love and we are all from the one divine light source.

There are a lot of inspiration writings in the world, but we wanted to write a clear basic message to you all. These messages will help and guide you and work alongside your day-to-day life.

As you read your chosen message, please remember you all have a guidance spirit team working with you, they are there to support you. Call upon them; they are there to help you.

Humanity has free will, so that is why you have to ask us; we will then send guidance down to you. Watch out for messages and signs from us in your busy day-to-day life.

Allow your inner light to shine.

Acknowledgement

You are all aware of the world around you, but there are areas in your life you are not acknowledging.

This could be a problem that you are not facing at work or home, a member of your family or a friend.

You are afraid of the consequences if you do face this area of your life and are trying to protect yourself from hurt.

You need to take this step forward, and deal with the situation; you will feel emotion, but once you acknowledge this pain and move through it, your whole world will become brighter.

We want your heart to be full of love again and your soul lighter. Do not carry the burden in your heart. Evaluate yourself, acknowledge the areas that need changing in your life and have faith in us – we are here to guide you.

Animal kingdom

You are a lover of the animal kingdom and feel broken-hearted when you see the ill treatment of animals on earth.

Your animals resonate with your souls; some are your guardian angels on Earth sent to look over you.

If you have not already, you will give many animals a happy, loving home.

Don't be afraid to give your heart to a pet because of past loss. They will always be in your heart and over the rainbow bridge in heaven, waiting to play again one day with you.

Enjoy, play and laugh with your pets and they will lift your spirit, keep you grounded and keep your heart young.

Be decisive

At the moment you are hesitating on your life's path. You are feeling indecisive about your future and what to do next.

You need to take control of your life, to shift the negative energy and move forward.

Hesitating is normal for humanity as it is a safety valve so you don't make mistakes. But you are afraid to take the next step in case it's the wrong one.

Have trust in your inner self-feelings; ask yourself which is the right decision for you.

You need some confidence at this moment in time. Look in the mirror and see your reflection, connect and think, "I am strength and trust my own choices."

Intuition is a gift for you all, so when you are indecisive, connect to this and the answers you need will be felt in your heart.

Be Inspired

Does the world around you inspire you?

Does just being you, inspire you?

What do you seek? You need to be inspired to seek your dreams.

Visit places that inspire you, breathe in the history of your world or other people's creations.

Take a walk in nature, observe and delight in Mother Earth.

Imagine your dream is your reality; search for inspiration and we will inspire your soul and help create your dreams.

Be true to yourself

Look into your inner being, it is pure spirit.

Being true to yourself and others helps our souls stay good and true.

Being true to yourself needs you to take time to reflect and look around you. Are you happy?

You might worry about making the necessary changes to your life and how it will affect others.

When you are true to yourself and happy, then others around you will be happier. You will attract the right people into your life and your spirit will feel lifted and energised.

Stay true to yourself, this will help you with your inner being, which needs to shine and be happy.

.

Challenges

From the moment your soul enters this world your life will be full of challenges.

Every challenge you face will help define you as a person and deepen your strength of character.

Draw on your inner strength to face these challenges.

You will find this within your heart and inner being.

As you rise to each challenge in your life, you will find strength, confidence and wisdom.

You are the challenge, you have what you need; reach inside for your strength, and rise above any fears – and shine.

Communication

Your voice is not being heard at the moment by the people near and dear to you.

Tell them how you are feeling, let out any emotion that might arise with this communication.

Talking to each other is so important in your busy life. If you do not do this, the negativity and worry will build up inside you. This needs to be released.

When you take the first step to make amends with a loved one or friend, do this face to face.

Let them see your eyes and how you feel. If you wait for others to break the silence you could be waiting a long time; it takes a strong person to make the first move.

Sing your tune to the world, let others hear your voice; you will only hear divine music all around you in your life as the communication flows.

Compassion

To be human is to feel compassion. You witness this daily in your lives around each other and in the animal kingdom.

Your heart stops and flutters at the violence and suffering in the world. Your inner being is deeply saddened by what you can witness on modern technology.

A simple gesture, reaching out your hand to a fallen friend, or holding them tight as they grieve in your arms is compassion. Saving a bee that's fallen into a pond or helping those less fortunate than yourselves is compassion.

If there is a time in your life when you need compassion, please accept it with grace, as this is a gift to help you heal on your life's path.

Be compassionate in your day-to-day life and this will help you with the understanding of your human journey on Earth.

Consequences

Consequences in your life start from the moment you take your first breath. People's actions and words affect you and your inner being.

You can be in the same situation as other people, but you will all respond differently, and your reaction will have consequences for those around you and the energy in the universe.

Think before you speak, as your words will affect others' feelings; some are more sensitive than others.

Look at how you behave in your day-to-day life. Be the best you can, live your life to honest and true values, be positive, and any action you take will have positive consequences for others.

Actions and words cause consequences that ripple through the universe; live in love and light and be aware of your own being.

Conclusion

Conclusion to you means a final solution, the end of a journey, a problem solved. But conclusion is much more; it has depth, knowledge and lessons learned in its meaning.

When you feel something is concluded, you move on with your life, but what will help you strengthen is when you reflect on what led to this conclusion.

Is it concluded? Are there unsolved feelings you need to resolve? Is there more you or others could have done? Or it might be as simple as reflecting on happy times with family and friends, what you love about them and your memories. It is important when you reach the final conclusion, you have no unsaid feelings and you are confident with the outcome.

We do not want you to hold bad energy and feelings in your heart. That is why it is important to take time to evaluate when you feel something is concluded. This will help you develop, and as you start to do this, it will become second nature.

Learn with every conclusion in your life.

Conqueror the world

As you travel you life's path on earth you may feel you are a tiny, insignificant dot and your self-worth is low.

Remember my friend, all of you, no matter what race or religion, are all as important as each other and we are all from the same loving light and are as one.

Each one of you makes a change to your world; every action you take resonates in the world's energy and affects it. Make your life's actions positive and loving, and you will attract this back to you.

Imagine the small dot you see yourself as spreading out around the world; as you imagine this, your energy and pride in your self-worth will grow.

You are you, you all are as one, and you all make a big difference and are loved and guided by us.

Connect with us and we will help your dot grow and conqueror the world.

Consideration

From the moment you understood your language you have been asked to consider others.

It can be perceived as a selfish act when you do not consider others' feelings and situations.

How do you feel when someone in your life does not consider your feelings or even your opinion?

Take time to step back and look at the people around you, imagine being in their shoes, what they are feeling and going through at that point in time. This is consideration.

Live your life considering others and ask to be treated in the same way. You will become a better person, have more understanding, and your fellow humans will learn from your considerate ways.

Teach this to your children and your grandchildren so the world is a better place for them to grow up in.

Development

From the moment you are born you start to develop the skills you need for your life's journey.

There will be a point in your life when you can take charge of your development and excel in what you want to achieve.

There is so much you can draw your knowledge from. There are teachers, books, your Internet, your parents, grandparents, friends, nature and animals.

You are a sponge, keep absorbing what you can on your chosen subject and you will grow and excel in what you do. As you develop, you will grow more confident. Some of you will become teachers of your chosen subject; this can be in education, a job role or a mother bringing up her child.

Everything you absorb goes towards your development and life's purpose. Go out into the world, my friend, learn, have fun while you develop, we will be here to guide and help you.

Empathy

Empathy is within you all. If you all looked on situations in your lives with more empathy then you would have better understanding of others and find forgiveness.

When presented with a picture in front of you, ask why the artist painted it, why they would use those colours and subject, what are they trying to express to you. Use this technique on situations that present themselves on your life's path; you will find you will start searching for answers and evaluate situations better.

When you live your life with empathy, answers will become clearer to you and you will better understand those around you. This way of thinking will become second nature to you; just think of the artist's picture rather than judge without thinking.

Think with your heart

Enjoy and play

To be content and happy within yourself you need to enjoy your life more. Enjoy your surroundings, your friends, your family, your work and just being you.

If there is an area of your life you do not enjoy, don't blame others, sit back and take a look at yourself. You can change this situation - just ask us and we will guide you.

Part of enjoying your life is finding time to play; as you relax and become more positive, positive changes will happen for you.

Take time for yourself, or a hobby, or go out into Mother Nature, walking and breathing in her healing love.

When you play you lift your vibration; this will then help you make any positive changes that need to be made for you to enjoy your life to the full.

Footsteps in the sand

As you travel your life's path you create your own footprints in the sand. But take a look behind you – they have faded in the sand as the tide washes in.

Don't try and retrace your steps and live in the past.

Accept the past, forgive, release any emotion and move on.

With the release of past anger and forgiveness your future footsteps will be clear and crisp.

As you take these new footsteps, learn to forgive as you move forward so you don't look back and try to retrace your steps, as they won't be there.

Time has washed your footprints away; they are just a memory that cannot hurt you.

Forgiveness

Forgiveness comes from the heart and soul.

Don't hold yourself back on your life's journey by holding on to emotions that cause negative energy in your inner being.

Release these feelings to the universe, lighten your burden, and as you forgive you make space in your heart and soul for new beginnings.

Positive energy will now fill your inner being; you will find it easier to forgive in the future.

Others will see your forgiveness and shining light and follow your example, the world becoming a happier place.

Gullible

Gullible is a term used in your society for those who have been taken in by another person, have over trusted them and been let down.

We know you have felt this in your life from the moment you understood the meaning of this word.

These lessons of broken trust are all part of your life's journey. If gullible means you have trusted wrongly then let it be.

You must never give up on that trust in your life. In trust you will find, hope, love, guidance and happiness.

Look for the good in any situation where you have been let down, rise above the negative and trust will be a day-to-day part of your life.

Healing

We do not know time in our world, but humanity needs time to heal.

Healing cannot be rushed, so take the time you need. Do not let others rush you? Only you will know when you are healed enough to step forward again in your lives journey and smile.

As you heal, you will carry on with your day-to-day life. Make sure part of this journey is communication, holistic healing and time out for yourself.

Your heart will lighten and every day will become easier.

Look in the mirror, smile and love yourself. Do not feel guilty for being happy again.

Your loved ones on earth and in spirit want you to be happy.

Have faith in yourself

There are times in your life when you will feel as if you are being tested and tested over and over again, pushed to your furthest limitations. You lose faith in others around you and yourself.

Take yourself back to a memory where you were at your happiest, note what emotions and thoughts come into your head from this memory. This is where we want you to be in your life.

Yes, challenges are placed on your life's path to learn from, but if you get into a pattern of negative thinking you draw negativity back into your life.

Have faith in yourself to change your life around. Start to reset your thought patterns; for every negative thought, replace it with a positive.

As you start to reset your brain to thinking this way, you will start to draw in positive energy and notice the world around you starts to become brighter. Your life's challenges will not be such a battle and you will overcome them. Believe in yourself.

Honesty

Honesty comes from within the heart. You all seek this from those around you.

Wake up each day and say: *"I will give honest answers from my heart and seek honesty from those around me."*

Honesty brings honesty.

It will inspire you to travel your path with this value in your heart.

Teach this to the children in your life so humanity can carry this value down the generations.

Honesty will bring truth; be true to yourself and live from your heart.

Humble

Feeling humble is a lovely natural feeling for humanity. Recognising the fact you are feeling humble means you know good from bad, and a compassionate nature and understanding.

You are a hard worker and help others. They see your qualities and admire you but you feel modest; you do not do these things for recognition and feel humbled when others admire you.

Take pride in what you do and achieve, you are all here for different reasons on your journeys.

Take the recognition and build on the energy it provides. This is positive energy and you will thrive on it.

Do not change the way you are; your kindness radiates round you and helps others. Yes, feel humble – we like this quality in you. Keep working and giving as you are, we are here to guide you and support your life's journey.

Intervention

It is time we intervene in your life's path; you have gone off track and need to be steered back onto the correct path for your life's journey.

As you read the first 3 lines, you know we are right and you now feel inner emotion. Let your feelings flow out, clear your negative vibes, take a deep breath and focus.

Step one: write down how you feel at this moment in time.

Step two: write down what you would like to be in your life and the positive way you want to feel.

Step three: how can you change your life's path?

Step four: what steps do YOU need to take to make this happen?

Step five: TRUST

Now you know what you need to do. Hand this all over to your guides and angels. Every day, read out loud the positive place where you want to be in life, and look for the help we offer as we work alongside you to make these changes happen.

Knowing

Your knowledge grows on your life's journey.

But you put up a barrier to obtaining this knowledge when you are negative and don't understand your own value and purpose.

When you lift in to a positive way of being, our knowledge and messages are there for you to read and learn from.

You will be amazed how the universe will open up to you and lead you to:

'Just Being You'.

Be confident in your own energy space and your lights will shine.

Laughter

Laughter is so good for your soul; it lifts your vibration to where it should be so you can feel happy with your life.

When did you last have a really good laugh and enjoy yourself? You need to be surrounded by light-hearted people and humor.

If there is no laughter in your life, you are at a stalemate point in your life's path. You need to look around you, shed the baggage that's dragging you down and step into the sunlight.

Say to yourself, *"I deserve laughter and happiness every day of my life and I will make this happen."* Repeat this 3 times a day to yourself; you will be surprised how you will begin to smile again.

Lighten your inner being with laughter and smiles.

Life's Journey

The first beat of your heart starts this life's journey.

Your path has been mapped out for you and as you take your first breath your journey begins.

You will have guides and guardian angels with you at all times to guide and help you on this journey.

We are listening and watching all the time; tune in to us to ask for help and guidance, we will answer and give you signs. This will be through written literature, your media, or a new person in your life, thoughts and ideas in your head.

You have free will and it is your choice whether or not to accept the guidance given. Remember we will always give our full attention and love to any thought and help you ask for, with the intention of helping you along the best life's journey.

You are here to learn and inspire your higher self, so enjoy this journey and let us walk along the path with you.

Lift your energy

For you to function well and be at your very best it is important your body energy levels are at their highest.

You need to look after your physical body better by making sure you eat a healthy, balanced diet. Research high energy giving food if you are very active. Daily exercise is very important for you – this will lift your mood, helping to bring stress levels down and bringing in more positive energy.

It is also important your inner spirit is energised too; you can achieve this with healing, meditation and grounding yourself. Also make time to do something in your life you love doing.

With a combination of the above you will be a new you. You will be lifted to a higher energy vibration, feel focused and be amazed at what you can achieve.

You are energy and you need to be at your best levels to achieve the best for yourself and those around you.

Listen

Take time in your busy life to sit in nature and listen to her song. Sit in a quiet meditative state and listen to your own heart and breath. Ask for guidance and hear our words of wisdom.

As you learn to slow down and focus, this will help you listen to others around you. At the moment, you think you are listening but you are not.

Ask yourself: *Are they sincere? Is there passion in their voice? Do they have honest intentions? Are they trying to guide and help you?*

Don't let your pride stop you listening and accepting their help. Use your intuition to decide what advice and help to accept.

As you start to listen you will find your life will open up, opportunities will arise, and that missing spark will reignite.

Make a wish

You make wishes every day, as you dream of better things in your life, or the lives of others. Make your wishes with true and good intent and the universe will hear you.

Don't worry about over-filling your wish pot, you can never have too many. But be patient, as wishes will be granted when they are right for you on your life's journey.

Your future is full of granted wishes; it will take time, but your wish pot will slowly empty and become reality.

So take the time to make a wish today and the universe will hear you.

Message of love

Love is in you; it is in your inner being, your heart, and all around you in Mother Earth.

We want you to feel this love, absorb its wonderful energy to lift your vibration.

You have so much love to give, just let it flow, don't let your past hold you back, you have enough love for everyone in your life and they need to see it.

As you give your love, accept love back into your heart, this will create the balance you need in mind and soul to be you.

Love your life; if you are not balanced in mind and soul then take time to reflect and make changes to help with this love transition.

The universe's energy is love, the basis of life is love, and we shine our love down onto you; feel our love's warm glow and shine love out onto your world and the universe.

Mind and body

Call upon Archangel Raphael to walk beside you daily to heal your body and mind.

When you are in physical pain or mental anguish ask for signs of how you can help yourself in your life to take the pain and worry away.

You need to re-access yourself and environment. Is it right and healthy for you?

When you know the areas that need improving, ask us to help you to take action to improve your life.

Rest your body as much as you can and in a quiet, meditative state ask for healing and guidance from Archangel Raphael.

When you see others suffering you can also call upon him to help and guide them too.

We will give you the strength you need. The angels want to help and spread our love, you are worthy of our help, so ask, we will be there walking beside you, giving you the best quality of life.

Moving forward

It is time to move forward with your life. You are holding on to grief and hurt from your past.

The emotions you feel could be from losing a loved one, a friendship, a pet or even a way of life you enjoyed. You will experience grief, anger, sadness, but now you need to experience acceptance.

With any type of loss the worst thing is to hold all the pain inside in your heart; let it go, release it to the universe. If you need support, seek counseling or a listening ear. Distract yourself with new friendships and find a new passion in your life. Don't be afraid to care again.

We are here, dear friends, to help you through this, ask us to support you along this journey to acceptance so you can step into your light again to shine and be loved.

We want to hear your laughter again.

Passage of time

As you follow the passage of time along your life's path, you will sometimes feel you are spiraling down a time tunnel, your life spinning out of control.

Reach out your hands to us and put on the brakes. It's at times like these you need to stop and evaluate your life and where you are in your life's journey. As you stop to evaluate, look around you, identify what's making your life unbalanced and spiraling out of control.

Write down what you want to achieve, what's stopping you and how you think you can improve this situation. Then give all these feelings over to the universe. We are listening.

Time will start flowing evenly again for you, lifting you into a positive place where you can achieve your life's purpose.

Remember – put on the brakes when the passage of time is spinning.

Passion

Your passion for life comes from within your soul and heart.

Life is full of passion for your lover, for creativity where your talents shine through, for reading, writing, nature, your job, your children, family, pets and life.

It is key to follow these passions in your life to get the best from yourself. When you achieve this you can then give your best to others around you.

Listen to your heart and see how you feel when you follow your passion in life. Your vibration is uplifted; your higher self resonates and shines.

Do not feel guilty about taking care of your own needs; when you shine, others around will too.

Follow the path of passion through your journey, find your inner self and shine out into the universe.

Protection

When you are feeling vulnerable and exposed to negative energies from those around you, call on Archangel Michael for protection.

He will place you in a blue light that will surround you for as long as you need it. Ask Michael to walk beside you, for strength and guidance. Give over to him the situations that are causing your self-esteem to be low.

When protected and feeling stronger, you will see the situations that cause you concern resolve, and your energies will lift, drawing more positive things in to your life's path.

Stand back, invite in Archangel Michael and you will feel your life change – negative energies will leave your body, drawing in new positive energies and beginnings.

Push through the mist

At the moment you are looking at the horizon and seeing a mist, and as you move forward this mist is not clearing. You feel as if you are waiting for a change in the wind direction then all will be clear. But the air is stagnant and the mist is thick.

You are what will make this change, so look inside yourself, and ask, what are your greatest strengths? When you recognise them, question yourself. Are you using them to the fullest you can in your life? Are you in the right job or relationship, where these strengths and talents can shine?

Once you see clearly the wind will change direction and the mists will clear. Once again there will be sunshine in your life, and others will smile at your happiness and new inner strength.

Ask your guides and angels to help with this transition in your life, we shower you with love and are listening.

Reach for the Stars

Happiness keeps you resonating, and your vibration strong and bright like the stars.

Your life will be faced with challenges that will knock you away from this place you all seek.

Obstacles are placed in your way on your life's path to challenge you. You will become stronger from these and this will enable you to reach inside for your inner strength to achieve happiness.

Allow yourself to be happy; you deserve this within your life. Look up at the stars when in doubt and feel their vibration resonating within your soul.

Reach for the stars and be happy

The world as one

You are all from one divine source and if you all worked together as one in love and light, what a wonderful, peaceful world you would live in.

You are all spiritual and healers, and as you take up this journey you will heal yourself and then teach this to others. Only you yourselves are holding mankind back, the part of you that does not believe or trust in us.

Connect with your inner being and higher self and when you feel comfortable with this and know yourself take the leap of faith and learn; you all have a life's mission to fulfill.

We will guide you to your path on this journey and work with you to develop your skills, but you must work hard and ask us for guidance.

Confidence and trust comes hand in hand. Look in the mirror and say, *"I can do this,"* and trust us, we will not let you down, we are here to teach you.

Our knowledge, love and inspiration is yours, trust and the rest will flow.

Trust in the stars

From time of old humanity has used the stars to guide them on their journeys, sailing the vast seas, climbing the highest mountains. No challenge was too much for them, as they trusted that the stars would guide them.

What direction are you going in at the moment – and who is guiding you? You all have a compass of life, you feel it is spinning and it needs to stop on a point of guidance. Just stop and look around you. Are you happy? Is there someone who is knocking you off course?

On a clear night look up at the stars, reflect on this and ask the universe for guidance. We are watching and listening.

Be brave and take that next journey on your map, don't try and sail the world in one day, take it port by port; listen to your inner self and trust in the stars, as we are giving you guidance.

Time to play

It is time for you to play and laugh, my friend. Lately you have been working hard and have not had much time for yourself, friends and family.

You need to take yourself back to the innocence of your childhood playtime, and find your inner child again.

This spark has been lost and when you reignite it, your soul will lighten and you will feel so much more like you.

Take yourself off to a place where you can relax, find a beach and build sand castles, have a kick around with a ball, do a hobby you are passionate about; playtime is your time, enjoy and relax.

You will know when you have back your inner child again – you will be more relaxed, you will look at life through a clear window, everything will seem brighter, laughter will be there again and the sun will shine in your heart.

Your inner child

Your inner child lies with your soul and higher self. When your inner child plays, sings and laughs then you are at peace and your spirit is lifted.

With the busy world you all live in this is sometimes suppressed and you are left lonely, waiting for a friend to knock and ask your inner child to come out and play.

This is such an important part of who you are – your personality, vibrancy and sparkle.

So take time to play, skip and run, have fun, be with loved ones – and your soul will shine, smile, laugh and be happy.

Sparkle

Your Journey

You have an old soul and have travelled many life journeys with us. You know this in your heart. You have a wise connection with the universe, and people are drawn to your wisdom and inner power.

You can be sensitive to others' feelings and know when they are not happy within their own lives.

You have a shining light that naturally wants to help others, but understand you will not be able to help everyone – sometimes they need to find their own path. Walk alongside them and be there if they need you.

You are spiritual, and healing is strong within you. Make sure you keep yourself healed and energised on this journey, and then others will gain from your healing light and wisdom.

Take a step forward and connect with us, we will guide and inspire your journey.

Your path

Continue on your existing life's path, as all will become clear to you in the near future.

You have felt that you have been branching off one way then another; this is not a test from us, it is just where you are now in your life's journey.

There are path signs placed along the way but you are not aware they are there. Ask us for guidance and help on making these decisions. We will deliver signs to you over the next couple of days, but you need to watch out for these, so keep us in your thoughts.

Sit in your own space with no distractions, feel your inner being, give your questions over to us on these decisions you have to make.

You will know with your inner intuition when you see the signs. Your path will then be clear to move forward without worry, but please look for the signposts of guidance for future decisions.

Wisdom

Your inner wisdom comes from centuries of knowledge across the universe. It is in each and every one of you; you just need to reach inside to find it.

As your life path grows you gain wisdom from knowledge, learning, making your own decisions, your world's spiritualists teachers and your history. From the moment you take a breath you make decisions; some will be mistakes, but from these mistakes you learn to make wiser decisions in your future.

As you grow older, you then become the teacher, passing this wisdom on to the younger generation in your life.

Live your life in wisdom, as this is key to a brighter future for you; your wisdom will pave the way for enlightenment and miracles in your life.

Walk a path full of wisdom and shine your light into the darkness.

About the Author

Sharon from Bengalrose Healing is a medium, author, holistic healer, spiritual teacher and mentor based in the United Kingdom. *'Heavenly Guidance'*, is part of a collection of books she has written, 'Utopia', *'The Magic of Words'*, 'The Magic of Spirit', *'Ayderline the Spirit Within'*, 'Step into the Mind of a Medium', *'Heavenly Guidance'*, 'The light within Atlantis', *'Your daily spiritual guidance diary'*, 'New Earth - The light beyond the horizon', *'The Celestial Guardians of Earth'* and 'Inspiration Guidance Cards'.

Sharon's books are available on Amazon, iBook's and https://www.etsy.com/uk/shop/Bengalrose

Visit her website www.bengalrose.co.uk to find out more about Sharon and what she offers.

Bengalrose is also on social media:

Facebook - www.facebook.com/SharonBengalroseHealing
YouTube - Sharon Bengalrose
Twitter - @SBengalrose
Instagram - BengalroseHealing

Sharon also welcomes contact through
email: Sharon@bengalrose.co.uk

Sharon is also the founder of the
'One Spiritual Movement' global community

Website - www.onespiritualmovement.com
Facebook - www.facebook.com/groups/onesm
YouTube - One Spiritual Movement

Twitter - @OneSpiritualMo1
Instagram - onespiritualmovement

Sharon also has a shop where you can buy spiritual items such as her meditations, books, and spiritual art.

https://www.etsy.com/uk/shop/Bengalrose

Printed in Great Britain
by Amazon